LOVE WHAT YOU DO...

and NEVER WORK a DAY in YOUR LIFE

LOVE WHAT YOU DO...

and NEVER WORK a DAY in YOUR LIFE

Always Wear Lipstick – Especially Red

PENNY SPENCER

Advantage®

Published by Advantage, Charleston, South Carolina.
Member of Advantage Media Group.

ADVANTAGE is a registered trademark and the Advantage colophon is a trademark of Advantage Media Group, Inc.

Printed in the United States of America.

ISBN: 978-1-59932-462-3
LCCN: 2014941246

Book design by Amy Ropp.

This publication is designed to provide accurate and authoritative information in regard to the subject matter covered. It is sold with the understanding that the publisher is not engaged in rendering legal, accounting, or other professional services. If legal advice or other expert assistance is required, the services of a competent professional person should be sought.

Advantage Media Group is proud to be a part of the Tree Neutral® program. Tree Neutral offsets the number of trees consumed in the production and printing of this book by taking proactive steps such as planting trees in direct proportion to the number of trees used to print books. To learn more about Tree Neutral, please visit www.treeneutral.com. To learn more about Advantage's commitment to being a responsible steward of the environment, please visit www.advantagefamily.com/green

Advantage Media Group is a publisher of business, self-improvement, and professional development books and online learning. We help entrepreneurs, business leaders, and professionals share their Stories, Passion, and Knowledge to help others Learn & Grow. Do you have a manuscript or book idea that you would like us to consider for publishing? Please visit advantagefamily.com or call 1.866.775.1696.

CONTENTS

ACKNOWLEDGEMENTS

I'd like to thank everyone who has supported me in the business and outside the business. My mother has been my mentor for as long as I can remember. And then my husband, the man behind the woman, who supports me, listens to me, and is always beside me.

I want to thank my children, for accepting me for being Mrs. Busy, as my daughter calls me. I also want to thank my staff for the loyalty and the support they have given me over the years. They have helped to make Spencer Group of Companies what it is today and have consistently gone the extra mile for our clients. I would like to thank my clients for allowing us to serve them and give them the very best and for the support they give my business.

I also wish to express my gratitude to my advisers: My accountant, John M., and my lawyers, Brett Oaten and Andrew Dawson. Because, at the end of the day, they are the key people who make up the big picture.

I could not do what I do without the help of all of these people.

INTRODUCTION

I wanted to write this book to share the reasons behind my success as Managing Director of Spencer Group of Companies, and also to let readers see the pluses and minuses of running a small business. Being a woman in a position of leadership and managing a family gives me a distinct perspective to successfully run a small business. Women tend to lead differently than men—not better—just differently.

The quick story behind my success is hard work and determination. I left home in New Zealand and came to Australia at 18 and was determined to get myself into travel. I was ready to spread my wings and leave home. I wanted to get out into the big, wide world. But it was hard to get a job in travel, and I kept knocking on doors and kept hearing "No. No. No . . ."

I took a travel course and then for six months volunteered my time at an agency stamping brochures. In the evenings, I waitressed in a nightclub to earn some money to live, so that during the day I could just work for free in travel.

It was really persistence, perseverance, and hard work. I was working all night and then getting up early in the morning, getting home at two or three in the morning from work, and then getting up at seven and going to work for free all day just to have my dream of working in travel. Finally, after six months, they employed me, and I had a full-time paid job in travel. It is still the same today. It's very hard to get into the travel business, because you can't get in without any experience. A lot of industries have internships, but the travel industry doesn't have that. You have to be lucky and find a company that takes in young people and trains them up, as I do now, in my business.

Spencer Group of Companies has very unique selling points. We offer knowledge and expertise. All of my consultants have been in the industry quite some time and have amazing knowledge. They will even remember the color of the bedspread in a hotel that they stayed at 10 years ago.

We offer impeccable service. It comes back to knowing the clients and giving them what they want, rather than what we think they need. It is walking in their shoes. Our consultants have traveled extensively. When a client says, "I've got to go to London," our consultant will advise and be creative; they are not order takers.

Spencer Group of Companies has a variety of clients, from holiday travelers to corporate executives and also the entertainment industry. We handle the travel arrangements for production companies that film commercials. Our client base is varied.

We cater to a specialized clientele. I'd had one production company client, and from that, it grew just from word of mouth and referrals. We had found our niche market. Once you have that expertise—and there are not many in the industry who have that expertise—the word gets around. If you do a good job, the referrals keep coming in.

CHAPTER 1

Spencer Group of Companies: What We Do and Who We Are

How We are Different from Other Travel Agencies

What we do really well at Spencer Group is innovate. I'm always open to opportunities. That is the key in businesses. You can't sit in your office and think that everything is okay. You have to look outside of that office and see what's happening in the city and globally, and really understand, not only your own business, but other businesses as well.

For example, we are an accredited space agent. We can sell tickets to space on Virgin Galactic. Now, that didn't happen just because I was sitting around thinking, "Business is good. I don't really have to look outside the square."

I read a lot. I talk to a lot of people. I'm in a lot of different groups. I'm on boards. All of that creates opportunities and innovation within my business.

How the Company Was Founded and Changed through the Years
"Work on the business, not in the business."

When we started, I had one other travel consultant working for me. I was consulting, and I had very long-term clients who just wanted to deal with me. Fifteen years later, I'm the strategist. I don't consult. I take clients out for dinner and lunches, I network with them, but I don't deal with them on a day-to-day basis.

That's really difficult for a lot of business owners, whether you're a hairdresser or a travel agent. You have dedicated clients who are there because of you, and when you can't deal with them anymore because you're growing your business and you have to get to that next level, you have to decide to groom someone up to be like you, so that your clients won't notice whether they're dealing with you or with another high level employee. You have to continue that progression throughout your company, as you grow.

I recently celebrated the 15th birthday of Spencer Travel. We had a big party, and one of my clients said, "Penny's created an office of Mini-Hers, like Mini-Me. They're all like Penny." I liked hearing that because that was my strategy.

I realized I wanted to change my role when I was heavily pregnant with my first child. I'd been in the business for about four years. I was sitting at my desk, still consulting and doing everything. I had swollen ankles and I could hardly walk. I thought, "What happens when the baby comes along? I can't do this." I had to take myself out of the business, and that was really quite difficult, but now I've never looked back.

It was hard, because it's like handing over a child. I was still in the business, but I wasn't doing that day-to-day work that everyone who starts a business is involved in. They start the business in the first place because they are good at what they do, whether it's the hairdresser, plumber, or even a lawyer.

You then get to a point where you realize you are good at what you're doing but now you have to run the business so it will grow. A lot of people might not realize this. They just stay the same and the business stays the same, but with most businesses, you need to grow. You do have to take yourself out of the business to some extent. Like the adage says, "You've got to work on the business, not in the business."

For clients, this transition was difficult. Because I was having a baby it made it easier for them. I was leaving them because I was having a baby, and that, to them, was acceptable because they thought I would come back eventually and be their consultant. But as time went on, I just handed over more and more to my other consultants.

I kept reassuring clients by saying, "I'm in the background. I know what's going on with your trip. I know what Lisa's doing. She's a great consultant." If you're just honest with them it will work out. I lost some clients along the way, but you have to make that decision.

Having children and running a business is a big commitment and requires hard decisions. When you start a business, it is like giving birth. I equate the business to one of my children because it does consume so much of my time. I love it, and it is hard when you start having a family and you have the business, the other child, making sure that you can give a bit to everyone. It is a juggle but it comes back to planning.

When I first came back into the business, after having my first child, I really struggled. I didn't know what my role was anymore. For 20 years, I had been a travel consultant, selling travel to my very loyal clients, and I came back into the business and wondered what I was meant to do now. I knew I had to be a strategist and run the business, work on it, not in it, but I didn't know how to do this. No one teaches you how to manage family life and a business.

My employees were very comfortable with my handing over more to them. I had a great team, including Lisa, who came with me when I started the business. She knew all the clients. That all went smoothly and the team was great with the change.

I employed a coach, and she really helped me get into the right frame of mind, because after having a baby you're so emotional. I went back to work very early after having Amy. She was only three months old. I was still breastfeeding and I was just an emotional mess.

I had the same anxiety that a lot of women get who go back to work early after having a baby. I was asking myself, "Should I really be doing this or should I just be an at-home mum?"

I'm a much better mother for being a working mother.

How I Learned the Business by Working for Others, Even without Pay

I have had some great employers throughout my career. I started volunteering with the owner of a wholesale travel agency business in Brisbane that sold adventure-type holidays. I will always be appreciative that he gave me that chance and gave me the role of receptionist after six months. I learned from the bottom.

I then came to Sydney and worked in another agency as what in those days was called a "Girl Friday." It would probably be called receptionist today. I did everything in the business from a junior perspective, and that was a great learning curve.

I moved up the ranks to a very large agency that was run by four men who were experts in their field. I learned a lot from that agency because there were so many great consultants. They had all the best corporate accounts in Australia. That's where I learned about service, because when you have high end clients, the service you offer has to be stellar. We did absolutely everything for these clients. If they needed a private jet, we'd organize that. It was all about service, and we were on call. In those days, there were no e-mails and no mobile phones, so you had to give them your personal phone number at home and you could be contacted at any time. That's just what you had to do.

I learned a lot in those early days. I then went to work for a woman who, unfortunately, is no longer with us. She was an amazing entrepreneur, and that's where I saw the entrepreneurial side of business. I was about 25 when I thought, "I really want to run my own business." Seeing a woman running that business made me realize, "Well, it's doable, as a woman." Before that, I'd always worked for men. It's was a different feel working for men, as opposed to when you work for women. The company had a different feel.

When I was working in those businesses run by men, it was back in the '80s. It was a very politically incorrect time. It was very much run, I felt, on how you looked more so than how you performed. Then, going to work for a woman, it was just so nice to be appreciated for who you are, not how you looked.

I left that agency after six years and then worked for another woman who started her own travel agency. I helped her start the business and grow it for four years, and then I left her and started my own. While she gave me the opportunity to learn how to start and grow a business, I learned a lot of what not to do, rather than what to do; for instance, how you treat people and how to win clients the right way.

There was a lot of competition for the bigger corporate clients. People would go in and undercut. It still goes on today. But I hold firm now. I know we're good at what we do, so I don't discount or cut fees.

When I left that agency, the last words the owner said to me were, "You'll never be successful because you have no integrity." That was like a red rag to the bull for me. I said, "I will be successful and I will show you how successful I'll be."

I actually bought that company last year.

Spencer Travel is definitely expanding. Focusing on business, first-class and corporate passengers is what we're good at. I have always loved high-end, and that's what I do. Again, it comes back to what you love to do yourself, and all the travel that I've done has been high-end. In addition, all my staff are very similar and have first-hand knowledge of high-end.

It is a very high referral business, because obviously even in the corporate world, if you have a PA to a CEO and you do a great job and she leaves, she'll always refer you when she gets to another company. That's how we win a lot of corporate business.

Tickets for Commercial Space Travel Are Available Now

Space travel is the new frontier and we're very excited about it.

I read an article, back in 2006, that Richard Branson was looking for travel agents in Australia to be accredited space agents. You had to write a submission about why you wanted to be an accredited space agent. I remember I spent the whole day, wrote this submission, sent it in, not really knowing what I should say, because I had never thought about selling tickets to space, but I just wrote very honestly about being innovative and looking at opportunities and moving with the times.

Then I got a phone call a few weeks later, saying that they were all coming to Australia and were going to interview some of the people who sent in submissions, and I was one of those people. They received about 200 submissions and they narrowed it down to 15. Fifteen presented to the panel, and I was one of the fifteen, then they chose eight out of that fifteen who had to give another presentation to the panel. I was very nervous and I had the flu. I never get sick, and I was sick as a dog. Two or three days later, they called me from London and said, "We'd like to appoint you as an accredited space agent."

We've sold four seats so far, at $250,000 US each. In the beginning, we weren't sure how to market it. Do we market it to the top 500 richest list? Do we market it to people who are into Star Trek?

But the reality is, you can't actually market it to a certain group. When I look at the people who bought tickets from us, you would just never think that they would buy tickets to space.

One is an orthodontist and is an adventurer. The other one was a Qantas steward, and he said he's been everywhere in the world but space. He wanted a ticket to space, and he downsized his apartment to buy it. The third person is an adrenaline junkie. The fourth one bought the ticket for his wife's 50th birthday.

We created our own website, SpaceTickets.com. Generally, when there's media coverage, or Richard Branson's talking about it in the press, people will Google it and they come through to the website. It's being part of the future—that is why we love being involved and being Accredited Space Agents.

A Small Business Should Specialize and Have a Well-Defined Clientele

A small business needs to have a defined clientele. There are three areas in a business: clients, staff and suppliers. For us in travel, the suppliers are the airlines, hotels, and wholesalers. And while all of these areas are important, it's really all about your clients. You don't have a business without them. The clients come to you. You can pick the clientele that you want and market to them.

Clients come to us because they like dealing with a particular consultant. The consultant gets to know them and gets to know what they like and dislike. There's nothing better than that service you get when you ring up and the consultant says, "Hi, John. Yes. Absolutely. I'll book you to London. I know you like seat 1A, and I'll get that driver, Don, to take you to the airport and pick you up from home at 7:00 a.m." We all love that. That's what the key is; making people's lives easy, and that's what we do.

Organization is Key

Technology is one of the biggest changes in the business. Fifteen years ago we had one computer with e-mail, and we would check that one machine in the morning and at night for e-mail. Fast track 15 years and we can get e-mail on phones and the TV.

Planning my time is a challenge. Technology has made us work harder. I loved the thought that we used to leave the office on a Friday, and have no idea what was going on until Monday, until you got those faxes on your desk. Now, you know every second what's happening.

I didn't want to have a BlackBerry, when they first came out. I thought, "I don't want to have e-mails on my phone," but I had to. My clients did, so I had to. Now, obviously, I have an iPhone, an iPad, and a mini iPad.

We have had to expand our staff with the new technology and have an IT department to manage the ever changing world of IT.

Being More Specialized Can Lead to More Clients

It comes back to expertise, definitely—knowing your client, knowing their needs. I've had a client who is married. I know his wife. I know what his wife likes to do, which spa she goes to, but I also know where he and his mistress travel to. We have to keep that confidential. You can become entrenched in your clients' lives; it comes back to building confidence in your relationships.

The clients' kids start booking with you. We even have third generations, where we've had the grandkids now booking with us. If the parent uses you as a travel agent and the children grew up knowing that Penny from Spencer Travel always booked the holidays, that can filter through.

We all travel extensively in our office, so that we know more than the clients, and I always say to my staff, "We have to be the ones who are giving them un-Google-able information." The only way we can do that is by traveling ourselves and being on top of destinations, hotels, airlines, because these change all the time. If a client can Google a hotel, well, why do they really need us?

CHAPTER 2:

Always Go the Extra Mile

Our tagline is "Above and beyond." We picked that because we always do go above and beyond for our clients. As far as going that extra mile, it's about doing more than just being an order taker and going beyond their expectations. And for me, it's about striving to be the best.

Have a Passion for Your Business

I have always had the passion for this business from day one, and over the years it has developed and grown. Keeping the passion alive in business is difficult at times because you're constantly on a roller coaster ride.

You have to keep on top of the simple things. Keeping yourself healthy. Remaining positive. Being able to just drive through the downs and run really well with the ups. I exercise every morning that gives me a positive frame of mind to start the day.

Sometimes it can be difficult to sustain that feeling, depending on what is happening in business or globally. September 11, 2001 was tough for everybody in the world. But when you're in business and in the travel business in particular, and no one's traveling, it was really hard to keep the passion and positivity going.

The Global Financial Crisis (GFC). That was another time where I just had to keep striving forward and making tough decisions. I was still passionate about my business so I went into survival mode.

Contingency planning is vital, and I had a plan that specified what I would need to do day by day. We lived by that contingency plan. Every day we would look at the figures, and then we would ask questions such as, if we didn't break even that day in revenue, how long could we sustain that?

If it was another five days, we would have to put another staff member on nine-day fortnights, or make someone redundant. We had a very specific plan based on figures.

I looked at the Profit and Loss and asked, "What can I cut?" It was the little luxuries like flowers that had to go.

I'll never forget. I went to the local nursery and bought artificial silk flowers, which I always hated. But the reality was we couldn't afford fresh flowers. We put people on short leave rather than letting people go because we were positive that there would be a turnaround. And when there's a turnaround, you are going to need good staff. But, eventually, we did have to let a couple of people go. The key sales staff were very happy to go on nine-day fortnights because they understood and wanted to keep their jobs.

I communicated with them daily, telling them that things were looking up, or that things were not so great, when they had to look at a week on or a week off as opposed to a day off. I kept the communication lines open so that they were never scared or unsure of the position of the company.

Running a Business to Be a Long-Term Success Requires Passion, Planning, and Connecting with Other Entrepreneurs

If you don't have a map, you don't know where you're going. And it's the same in business. Your plan is your map. It is best to always have an annual plan, a 5 year, and 10 year plan.

For eight years I have been part of the Best Practices Group that includes nine other travel management companies. We get together every quarter and go through our figures, analyze, and determine the best practices that work within our industry and with each business.

That definitely has helped me get through difficult times because the group includes other travel agency owners. Most of the time they're going through what we're going through because travel is quite cyclical.

Planning is important, but so is having the support of like-minded people. Getting out of your comfort zone at times is very important as well. I know a lot of people hate to get out of their comfort zone but it ensures growth.

The Best Practices Group has a facilitator who takes our quarterly financials and analyzes them. He then puts them into a very large spreadsheet and when we get together we spend the whole day analyzing each other's numbers and financials.

We also go through the business and visit the offices of a member. They do a presentation on their business, which we critique and offer suggestions on what and how they could improve their business.

It's very worthwhile, although, at times, it can be confronting; it helps you grow because you learn.

This group is for travel agents and, while it means getting together with your competition, like everyone always says, "Keep your enemy close." There have been times where a corporate account has come across our desk who I know deals with one of our best practice group members. I'll ring that other agent and say; obviously this client's not happy. Maybe you need to go and visit them." It's an unwritten rule between us.

I'm also part of EO, which is the Entrepreneurs Organization. This is a little bit different from the Best Practices Group. EO is a group of entrepreneurs from different industries and we meet once a month. There are so many different skills that you need in a business that sometimes come out more in other industries.

Again, being surrounded by "like minded business owners," but a lot more broad.

Automated Access so Clients Can Monitor Itineraries, Expenses, Bookings

It is essential to keep up with technology and stay informed about what will help make our lives and our clients' lives easier; as well as which new innovations will increase the productivity of the staff.

We are constantly looking at IT to check that we've got the right technology. Things like SMS-ing the clients before they leave to say, "Have a great trip." Keeping in touch with them while they're away. Putting ourselves in the shoes of the traveler. Making sure that everything on the itinerary is correct.

Some of our consultants will actually follow the client's itinerary throughout their journey. If the client is going from Sydney to London, leaving Sydney today, he or she will arrive in London tomorrow. So today we will ring the hotel in London and make sure that the hotel knows that the guest is a VIP, that they've got the room with the balcony, all those extra bits and pieces. Going the extra mile. We continue doing that step by step throughout the itinerary.

All of my consultants are very well experienced and knowledgeable so they know travel. We've all done what our clients are doing. So we can easily say, "Oh, look, when you get off in L.A., you know it's going to be a nightmare with customs. You're not allowed to use your mobile phone. So don't switch it on."

As for the mobile phones. SIM cards don't work in Japan. So we always tell clients going there that they need to get a different SIM card. This makes the difference in whether the client can use their phone when they get to their destination because we have prepared them for that.

We match the consultant with the client. Some clients can be very high maintenance and require a lot of hand-holding. So there are certain consultants, obviously, who are more inclined to do that. When we do the initial consultation with the client and we win the business, we get a good idea of what kind of client they're going to be and can tailor our services specifically to their needs and desires.

CHAPTER 3:

Mentoring: Learning and Teaching

Having a Mentor

I have been both a mentor and a mentee. In the early stages of my business, when I realized that I needed help, I joined the Australian Businesswomen's Network, a government mentoring program. The mentor/mentee relationship is about a transfer of knowledge. Someone who's been there, done that, guiding you through whatever you need and that was what I needed at that time.

When I was accepted into the six-month program, which is funded by the government and Westpac Bank, I was matched with a mentor. This helped me in that next stage of the business. Two years in, I was working so hard, I didn't have time to even look at what the next stage was in my business. So when you sit down with your mentor, they guide you through and help you with getting to that next level.

I currently have a mentor. You should never think you know it all. There's always something new to learn. I have a $40 million business that is successful and has won awards. Obviously I'm doing a good job.

Now what? And that's why having a mentor who's that level up from you is essential. I'm learning things from him now that I would never have thought of: how to get onto boards, more about mergers and acquisitions, what's happening in the global markets in travel and how I can tap into that. People might think because I'm successful I don't need to keep trying to improve. But that's why I'm an entrepreneur.

In the past, my mentors have pushed me when I needed to be pushed. One of my mentors introduced me to awards. She said one of the ways to be successful is to win awards and nominate yourself for awards because it takes you through a process. The process alone makes you realize how much you have accomplished.

You learn a lot from doing the submission. Then you learn from going through the process of presenting to a judging panel. It can build your confidence. And then when you win, it's fantastic. I probably never would have thought of doing this. She pushed me and now I submit three or four awards a year.

Being a Mentor

Three years ago I started the not-for-profit Travel Industry Mentor Experience (TIME). I felt the travel industry needed a mentor program specific to the industry. We've put through 50 plus graduates in those three years. It's working well and I'm very proud of that.

While being a mentor doesn't help my business as such, it does help the industry. Because I have such a passion for the travel industry, I want to ensure that we still have professional people in the industry, that we still have people who want to work in the industry. In five or ten years' time, who's going to be the next Penny Spencer?

That's one of the key reasons why I started TIME. I also wanted to give back because I have had so much wonderful help and knowledge transfer from my mentors.

This works for other types of businesses as well. Anyone who is starting in business needs a mentor. Life coaching is very different from mentoring. Mentors have the experience and transfer that experience and guide you. Coaching is more about coaching you through the process. It might be about what you're going through at the time, not necessarily about your future and your vision.

Mentoring is about taking you to that place that you want to go. It's a work in progress. Our industry can be lazy. A lot of owners of businesses in the travel industry in Australia aren't willing to train their staff or invest in their staff. And that's one of the problems in our industry and another reason why I started the mentor program, because you've got to train people or at least give them some help and guidance along the way. When people ask me, "What if I train them and they leave?" I always say, "What if you don't train them and they stay!

CHAPTER 4

Connect with Others

TEC, The Executive Connection, is another group I have belonged to. This is a group of CEOs and we get together monthly. It is very similar to EO; however, it's CEOs, whereas EO is about entrepreneurs. TEC took me on a great journey. It took me to a different level because I was sitting in boardrooms with CEOs of large companies, and sometimes global companies, and I really had no idea how those levels of companies operated compared to my company.

We weren't allowed to be in the same industry. No conflicts. I was in TEC for four or five years and I learned a lot. I used to walk into these rooms and feel completely intimidated. TEC took me way out of my comfort zone and gave me a lot of confidence.

I realized that if I could sit in a room with these people who are 10 times above me at that stage in my career, learn from them and hold my own, after a couple of years I would feel like I was one of them. That would be a huge achievement.

I learned so many skills from these groups. I definitely have a much better understanding of the financials. Because at TEC, I used to say, "I feel like I'm being undressed in front of you all." We had to put our financials up every month and go through them and explain to the other members. Why I had a loss or why I made a profit and how.

Before TEC, I used to read the P and L and the balance sheet and understand it somewhat, but never drilled down into it. I gradually became much more comfortable, and a lot more confident. I gained confidence also in public speaking because I had to stand up every month and go through the nuts and bolts of our business to other CEOs.

EO is more entrepreneurial while TEC got me through to a much higher level.

It's different when it's your own money that you're putting into your company. That's why I'm enjoying Entrepreneurs Organization. We all started from scratch, built up our business, and enjoy the roller coaster ride together.

Both organizations are different; however, both bring something that's valuable for my business. I would recommend these organizations to any business owner because they take you out of your comfort zone. That's what you need to do to keep learning and growing.

You Cannot Go It Alone. Surround Yourself with Like-Minded People

You can run a business by just sitting in your office and doing what you do every day, but then you're working in the business, not on it. It's so important to get out and actually start talking within your industry as well as with other industries.

You can become very insular about your own industry, so you have to step outside of your own sector and learn from other people in other industries. All industries have clients, staff, and products or services to sell.

Meeting with people outside your industry can help with many issues, such as software decisions. Quite often, when you're in your industry you only use industry-specific software.

Working with others in EO, I have found out about different CRMs, for example Zoho. We were using Salesforce because that's what everyone in our industry uses, and then one of the EO members told me about Zoho, and how it costs much less yet does all the same things. So I looked into it and he was right. I was paying $10,000 a year and Zoho is $750 a year and it works for all industries. I would never have even known about it. So I think stepping outside of your industry is a good thing.

It's amazing, the people that you meet along the way. I was working for a family-run company which taken over by Thomas Cook, which was a large, global company. The woman who was employed to come in and deal with that takeover, change and sort out the staff from Thomas Cook's point of view, was someone everyone feared.

When there is a takeover, you're never sure if you're going to keep your job. She came in and ruffled everyone's feathers. She gave me my first evaluation, which was very confronting.

As time went on, this particular woman has become, not only one of my coaches, she's helped me with particular projects. When I first started TIME, the Travel Industry Mentor Experience, she came onto the board immediately and she and I have run that not-for-profit organization together.

She's now a great friend and throughout the years, she has taught me a lot. She coached me when I came back from my first maternity leave, on how to get back into business mode from being in mother mode.

From someone I was nervous to be around, she has become a big part of my business and also a friend. You just never know the people who can help you along the way. Don't dismiss people, look beyond what you see.

Organizations Give You Accountability

When you work for yourself, there is no accountability. If I walk out of work at night and announce that I'm going home to do my business plan, when I walk in tomorrow none of my staff are going to ask me if I did the business plan. Having been part of business groups gives you that accountability where you're accountable to them. At EO, if you don't achieve your goals in a month, you get fined $20 per goal. Having accountability is key when running a business and helps you get things done that you may usually sit on.

Conferences

Conferences are important for self-education. EO has different conferences that you can attend globally and within Australia. They call them universities because it's about learning.

I could be at a conference all year round. There are the travel conferences and the different trade shows. I'm on the Shangri La Global Advisory Board, so I travel a bit with them as well. I tend to pick one or two per year, and one EO per year.

For me to take the time to attend, the conference has to be of a certain level. It's got to have good speakers and other attendees who are of the same caliber as me. People ask me if I choose based on the destination. I would much rather that they all be in Sydney. Last week, I went to a conference in Noosa, which is lovely and has a beautiful beach. But I never saw the beach because I was in a conference room the whole two days. I can get to some very glamorous places but never see them. The criteria is about the content. I also have to consider how long the event is because I can't be out of the office for more than a week at a time. It's all about what I'm going to learn and who I'm going to meet.

Some Conferences that Resonate:

From a travel industry perspective the annual Virtuoso Travel Week in Vegas stands out. Four thousand people were part of it last year—all suppliers and buyers. Eight hundred appointments and four days of four minutes per appointment.

What you learn is incredible, as well as the people you meet. You're mingling with the GMs of the best hotels in the world. I met the owner of a company in Turkey when I was there. She does lots of unique itineraries in Turkey and we had a trip there for a family, and you can't rent baby seats in Turkey. I phoned the woman I'd met in Vegas and explained that her company was doing a huge itinerary for us but that we needed baby seats. She told us not to worry. She would borrow one from her sister.

Another example of how the people we meet make a difference to our business is we had clients trying to go to the Cannes Film Festival. They booked late. Cannes is completely booked out for the film festival but because I had met the GM of one of the hotels at Travel Week, I phoned him and he said, "Leave it with me. I'll get you a room."

It's these things that wow our clients. And if we're not attending those sorts of events, we don't get to meet those people and we can't impress our clients and exceed their expectations.

Staff and Conferences

It's important to send your staff to these events and we do quite a bit of that. I took two of my managers with me to a conference I recently went to. I took three staff to the Travel Week in Vegas. It depends on the conference and the timing. We send staff to conferences on their own as well, based on what the conference is.

We would probably send 12 to 15 staff away a year to conferences. We rotate which staff attends the conferences. They learn from it, and they meet people who they can use day to day in their job.

Staying connected is very important. It's about the networking and self-education.

CHAPTER 5:

Dealing with Change

How September 11 and the GFC Affected Business and How We Coped

September 11 and the GFC were both big change components for us in travel and for everybody. Our business was affected by 9/11 for six months.

Our phone was ringing madly, but it was people calling about cancelling their flights and getting refunds. Everyone was panicking. Once we'd managed all of that hysteria over the next couple of days, the phones just stopped ringing. I had to look at what areas we could go into that didn't involve international travel.

At the time, we were doing a lot of US TV commercials. So I had a lot of US TV crews coming out to Australia filming. Not only would they fly around Australia, but fly out from the states, bringing actors, crew, and staying in hotels for two or three months. It was a large income for us that just stopped; it stopped for a couple of years.

We had to look at how we could grow the domestic market. I contacted our existing corporate clients, knowing that they wouldn't be traveling internationally for a while, but focusing on their domestic, which probably at that time they were booking through the internet, which seemed convenient and less expensive. That's what I could see as something that could get us through that next stage of no international travel. I concentrated on the domestic travel, and worked with production companies in Australia to do domestic travel or maybe across the Pacific or the Trans-Tasman region.

To do this we had to sit down and come up with ideas of how to ensure the business survived. At the time, we didn't know how long the whole scenario was going to last because of the security. Every day there was a new situation about security and clients were saying it was too hard to travel, too much security, and that they were too scared. It was a tough time for everybody.

I had a smaller business then, with eight or nine staff. I did have to let a couple of people go and then concentrate on finding new ways to do business. I was pregnant at the time with my first child, so a lot of my clients were in the throes of me transferring them across to other staff. Amy was born in April, so from September to March was when I readjusted the business by looking at new markets and also readjusting it for me not being there for the next three months.

In business you don't know what's going to happen every day. It's very different from having a job where you know what you have to do that day. In business anything can happen. For example, yesterday I had a planned day and it went completely pear-shaped because certain people needed to talk to me about certain things, so my day was spent in meetings as opposed to doing what I had planned to do. Life is erratic when you own a business. You can't always say, "I'm going to get to do what I want to do today." That was certainly the case with both September 11 and the GFC. You have to concentrate on key issues when needed.

Be Prepared for When the Schedules and Plans Go Awry

I have an open door policy in the business; anyone can come in and talk to me at any time. I do request that they send me an e-mail or text, or use our intercom and ask if they can see me that day or, if it's not urgent, the next day, and to give me an idea of what their issue is.

Not long ago when I got in, there were quite a few messages from people wanting to talk to me about things that were urgent. I really had to put aside my schedule and fit them in around whatever was on my schedule for the day. With days like these I have to stay back to get through the work I missed.

How we Adapted When Airlines Stopped Paying Travel Agencies Commissions

Another change in our industry we had to adapt to was when the airlines stopped paying commissions to travel agents. It had happened in America, and what happens in America usually happens to us two or three years down the track.

The airlines were not going to give us a percentage at point of sale. Before, we'd get a percentage when we issued a ticket.

We also would get an override, which is an extra payment based on our targets with the airline. When they stopped paying that point of sale commission, the money that we had been earning halved. We had to restructure the whole model. It affected the entire travel industry. A lot of people found it difficult to start charging their clients fees, and the clients found it difficult to understand why, for so long they'd got free service from us, as travel agents, and now they had to pay us, like a lawyer or an accountant.

It was in the message to the clients. As always, I believe in transparency and honesty. I don't try to hide anything. I explained the situation to my clients and brought it back to their business as well. The key to discussing change with clients is relating it to their business. Whatever industry they are in, how do they make their money?

If you're talking business owner to business owner, that's okay. But some of the larger corporations, of course, weren't particularly thrilled because it's all about the bottom line and shareholders. You have to give them a different message and talk about the service that they're going to receive for the money. And if they're not paying a service fee, they're not getting any service. It involved restructuring the whole model, and communicating with the clients.

A lot of clients think, I'm not going to pay that fee. I'll just do it myself. And then they realize when they make an error on a travel site on the web, such as they didn't get a visa when they were going to Vietnam, because the Internet site didn't tell them, they come back to us and they're quite happy to pay the fee.

We had to analyze our systems, how our staff was doing things, and what we could do to improve on that productivity so that there's a productivity gain. If they're making a booking in five minutes, we're earning $40 on that booking and they're only being paid $30 an hour. It's an economy of scale whereas before we probably didn't have to worry as much, because we were making good money on bookings since we were making the commission at the point of sale. The difference now is we only make a service fee at point of sale. We have to wait three months for the growth target incentive payment.

Adapting Your Business

It is also dealing with change with your staff as they change. When they get married, have children, etc. you have to adapt to that. A good example is Lisa, who came across with me when I started the business from the other agency. She was a key part of the business who went on maternity leave.

She wanted to come back part time and we were very much corporate and entertainment travel at that point. You can't consult part time for this type of business because you have to be there all the time. I decided I'd start an area for her for travel with kids. She was now a mother, it was a market that people really needed, because traveling with kids is completely different than traveling on your own or as a couple.

I created a Travel with Kids division and set her up so she could work three days. This was something she could relate to, now having children. Her children were now school age and since she lived quite a way away from our head office, I set up an agency for her in her area. This was Shire Travel, and she didn't have to commute anymore and she could build a community-based business.

That business is now highly successful. If you have good key staff, it's important as their life changes, to look at your business and how you can match improving your business to their life changes.

Carissa, one of my other staff who's had her second baby, is going to run a new agency close to her home for me. I've got another woman who has two children and works from home three days a week.

Another one of my staff who worked for my 24/7 business, was fantastic. She left because that job was tough. It's tough to work in a business where people are always yelling at you because it's an emergency mostly when they call.

She had a period where she said, "I just can't do this anymore." So, she left and went off to another role. And then, when she left that role, she called me and she said, "You know what? I want to come back. Not necessarily to 24/7, but I'd like to come back to Spencer Group of Companies.

I started a groups department for her. All along the way, you evolve different businesses for different staff, based on their life changes, and it pays off for the staff and the business.

Helping Staff to Flow with Software Changes

Sometimes there are issues with updating software and implementing new systems with staff. Most of my staff have been with me for a long time, so they know that we're an innovative company. And they know that we're always moving forward.

There are lots of different software options that we've found just by asking other people and seeing what other people are using. Our equipment, processes and systems are easily accessible. The CRM system is another area that we've worked quite hard on to make sure that our database is up to date. If we want to send out an interesting piece to our clients about something in travel, we can do that in two minutes with our database and our CRM software.

Our sales staff have three screens. This is a productivity gain of 35 percent. They have their e-mails on one screen. The reservation system is on the other screen and either the internet or the back office is on another screen. They can literally work through a booking in five minutes.

It's looking outside the square to ask how we can do things better. Recently, I had multiple conference calls trying to win the business of a global account whose head office is in Seattle. They wanted a very specific report because they needed to download it into their global expense system. There was no software for a report anywhere like that, so we created it for them. I contracted a systems analyst and she sat for two weeks designing a macro to create this report that we could download for them. We won the account because of that.

CHAPTER 6:

Mergers & Acquisitions: Not Just for Big Corporations

Mergers and Acquisitions are opportunities. It's looking for opportunities or being open to opportunities. I've done a number of different mergers and acquisitions. The first was a company that was closing down their travel department. It was a large shipping company and they had started a travel side because a lot of their clients use their ships for cargo. The shipping company thought, they're using us for cargo, why don't we start a travel company and they can use us for travel?

They operated for a few years, but then they realized it wasn't their core business and went in search of a travel company that would take over those clients.

By having a high profile within your industry you are more open to opportunities. All of my opportunities have arisen because I am visible in the media, at functions and it is evident that my company is in a growth phase. When any opportunity arises, people call you.

This particular company contacted me and said they wanted to hand over their travel company to someone, and was I interested? That was unusual because there was actually no financial gain for them. They wanted us to go out to all their clients and give them a travel company to deal with. There was no guarantee that those clients were going to book with Spencer Travel.

It was a hard sell. This company was backing us and going out with me to their clients and telling them that it wasn't really a merger. The clients were merging across to us but we weren't purchasing or taking on the other company. There were 30 clients worth $5 million, and we managed to get $4 million, and we've retained $3 million, which was five years ago. Don't be scared to look at different ways to acquire business.

How a Small Business Can Get in the Merger Game

Any small business can make it known that they are looking for acquisition opportunities. They can talk about it in the industry, they can employ a broker. But the best way is word of mouth. I get many businesses sending me their Requests to Sell. The more that you get across your desk, the more you learn about business and about acquisitions, because you see so many different businesses and so many different financials.

First, why are they selling? Usually it is because of retirement, and if it is, have they built the business up or have they let it run down? If you want to sell your business, you have to plan for the sale 10 years before you actually want to sell it. If you're 40, and you know at 50 you don't want to be working, you need to plan at 40 to sell by 50. *(I go into that in more detail in Chapter 14: Have an Exit Strategy Right from the Start).*

Because if you say, at 50, I'm tired of this now, I want out. Too late. You're sick of it and you've probably run it down. And it won't be sufficient for sale. A lot of businesses end up shutting their doors. No one will buy it, because it's not a viable business.

It comes back to planning. If you're going to sell, you need to plan for it. You can't wake up one day and say, I'm sick of this. I want to sell. And that's what I see a lot of—people ringing me saying, I'm so tired, and I'm 60 now, and I really don't want to do this anymore. Would you be interested in buying? When you get the financials, you can tell that the love is no longer in that business. The passion has gone.

Prepare Yourself and Your Company to Be Able to Take Over or Merge with Another Business

First, you need to have the right infrastructure. I've built the infrastructure over 15 years. We have an accounts department. We have an IT department. I have managers. It's very appealing when you first look at a four-man business and the owner's doing the books. The husband's probably trying to work out the IT, and the owner is managing. Then all of a sudden, the owner says, I'm going to sell this business. There's no one doing the books. The husband's gone as well, so there's no one doing the IT. And there's no one managing.

If you were to buy a business like that without your own infrastructure, you'd have to employ another three people. It's not viable. If you have your own infrastructure and a head office scenario, you can buy that business, bring the IT and the accounts into our head office, and the management comes from my managers within, so I don't need to spend any more money by employing extra staff. If I buy that business for, maybe $100,000, I don't have to add in three more salaries because I've already got the infrastructure to manage those areas.

Dealing with Different Business Cultures in Takeovers

Some owners want to stay in the business because, in travel, they want to consult and not manage. That can and can't work. It really depends on the person. It's hard to know when you buy a business how that person is going to react to being managed by someone else when they were always the key person making the decisions.

The other option is where the owner doesn't want to be in the business at all and gets out. Then you can create your culture with the existing staff.

We do many things when we buy a business. We have a welcome dinner with all the staff. My managers will spend days in their office. We will bring them into our office to spend time with us. We have staff conferences where we all get together. We have the Christmas party where they bring their partners. We also have a staff appreciation dinner in the middle of the year, which brings all the staff together. When you have lots of different locations, it's hard to create the same culture at all locations.

M&A: Think before You Leap

Going into any merger or acquisition, ensure you have done the due diligence. This is very important. I've been looking at another business and I've been working with them or their broker for the last four or five months, just on due diligence, before I even make an offer. That's really important when you're looking at mergers and acquisitions. It may all look good on paper, but you can't be sure until you actually drill down and get into the business. Due diligence is about asking the real questions.

Get in on the M&A, Even if You Are a Small Company

It comes back to growth. Every side of the business has to adapt and grow—our incentive scheme is all targeted to growth. A business has to grow to keep making money. Sometimes it's difficult to keep growing. Every year you grow and the next year the suppliers want more growth.

You have to grow to keep earning money. In the travel industry it's difficult to grow organically, unless you have a Business Development Manager and a very strong plan of growth. Most of the time when I look at how can I get that extra five million, I may see if there are some smaller agencies that have a five million dollar turnover that I can take over or buy.

It's having the right infrastructure and having some cash flow. You can't buy businesses unless you're making a profit yourself and have some money to purchase the business.

The strategic areas to look at after purchasing the business are how to retain the key staff and the key clients. Look at the investment areas in the business, improvements and upgrades, and the productivity gains and improvement of policies and procedures.

Branching Out: Stay within Your Core Industry

I have learned to stay within the core business. I've branched out to 24/7 Solutions. I started that business, which is selling an after-hours service to other travel agents. Although that's not selling travel, it's still within the travel industry, a sideline to travel.

I could buy a business like a florist or a bakery. I know I could do that, just because I know I have the expertise financially to work out whether it would be viable or not. While all businesses are basically the same, I don't know those industries. I realize that a lot of entrepreneurs buy and sell and it doesn't matter what the business is. I personally think it's better to stay in the industry that you know. That's because I've always been in that one industry.

And again, that's where my passion is.

I started 24/7 Solutions because corporate travelers need 24-hour service. A lot of owner-managers were doing their after-hours service themselves or giving existing staff a mobile and a laptop. Probably 10 years ago that sufficed. As the needs of corporate travelers grew, they needed a more professional service. I had a couple of employees doing my after hours. They both resigned on the same day. I was eight months pregnant with Charlie. None of my staff could do the after hours. I had to think really quickly. I decided to start a business that would offer this professional service, a professional service not only for Spencer Travel, but also for other travel agents. I couldn't take on four staff, invest in the technology that I needed, and just have it for Spencer Travel. It wasn't going to be viable financially.

It's been tough. There was never a model for this sort of business in Australia. Some of the other large corporate companies use services overseas, switching their phones over to South Africa or to London. The problem was that when a corporate traveler called and said, "I need to go to Albury-Wodonga," someone in South Africa didn't know where that was because they didn't know Australia. They'd know if the traveler said, "I'm in London and I need to get back to Sydney" that's a simple process.

I hired four staff. I had them working remotely and on a roster basis. For the first three years it was really tough. We've broken through. We're into the sixth year, and we're now making a profit. It's starting to stabilize. We've got 40 travel agents utilizing our service.

It's about looking at the bigger picture, not just looking at the problem right now. Go beyond that. That's what I did. It was a huge risk. I have called that business my difficult child. Staffing it is challenging. The technology was a huge investment. Selling it to other travel agents as me, their competition, was difficult. We've finally come out the other side. We now have agents calling us and saying, "I need an after-hours service. We've heard about yours. Can I sign up?"

When I'm given a problem, I sit back and look at the bigger picture. That's entrepreneurial.

CHAPTER 7:

Partnerships

Partnerships are more about choosing the right partners as alliances or affiliates within your business.

It's the same as buying a business. Its due diligence, making sure that your partnerships enhance your business and that they are the right fit. It comes back to relationships. In travel, you really need to have a buying group to be able to get the best deals.

There are different buying groups. The bigger the group the bigger the buying power with the airlines and the suppliers.

Some of the buying groups are more about quality rather than quantity. Although they might have 30 travel agents within their group, those 30 travel agents might just do all business and first-class travel so their yield is very high, as opposed to having 100 in a group that only do economy packages.

How did I pick my buying group? Well, again, it is doing the due diligence and making sure it is the right one, with the right-minded people.

It comes back to the whole idea of working on your business, not in your business. If you're constantly just dealing with day-to-day issues within your business and not looking at the big picture, you can get stuck with affiliations that really aren't right for your business and where it's going.

There are also partnerships with suppliers. The Four Seasons Preferred Program invited us into a partnership because we produce so well for them. Now that's a great fit because our clients love Four Seasons and we now can offer so much more to our clients from being in this program. Having the right partnership also benefits your clients.

Don't necessarily just look locally at your partnerships. We're affiliated with Virtuoso in the States, which is a large luxury network, and that has done a lot for our business as well. It's not just about looking in your own backyard. It's about looking globally at what other affiliations and partnerships can enhance your business.

CHAPTER 8:

Employees: How to Inspire

Having happy employees is all about having the right culture and you have to work on that. A lot of businesses now have a great culture. When you ask them "What makes a great culture? What did you do? How did you create the culture?" They can't really answer you. The culture is key.

It's taken our business the full 15 years to say that we have a culture that works. Not only is it about that culture, it's about the type of people that your culture brings into the business. I now have people e-mailing and phoning me saying they want to work at Spencer Travel because they've heard about what a great place it is and the culture's amazing.

First of all, you've got to create a culture through your values and then you've got to walk the talk. It's a bit like building a website. You build a website, but you've got to get people there. It's the same as building a culture. You build a culture, but then how do you get the message out and attract the right people to that culture?

Over the last 15 years, employees have come and gone. Some I've let go. Others have not wanted to be within our company for different reasons. It's not one size fits all. It's not until you really have that strong culture that you know the sort of people that you want on the bus.

Think about a bus or a train that has three carriages. You have the front carriage. We draw and put who's in the front carriage of the train. These are the people that are 100 percent committed to your business and are loyal and do the right thing and have amazing work ethic. They're all in the front carriage.

The second carriage of people are those who you can move up into the front carriage. They're on the way. They just need a bit more help. The third carriage is anyone who is not on board. We go through this every six months. Whoever is in the third carriage, we generally let go. The third carriage can derail the first two carriages.

We live by that. In the beginning of the business you're almost afraid to get a reputation out there that you sack people or people leave. You don't like to think you have a revolving door in the business. Over time I've learned that it's better to just lose the people that aren't on board than keep them because you're afraid of your reputation. If you keep them, your reputation gets worse and you could lose performing staff by keeping the non-performing staff.

Getting along with Employees

I treat people the way that I want to be treated. I like to have people around me who are honest, who have passion, who are committed, who are loyal. That's what I look for. First of all, obviously, we look for skills. I always say to my managers, "You can't train attitude." If they've got all these skills but they don't have the right attitude, or they don't fit our culture, there's no point in employing them.

How to Recognize Who Is a Fit

It is hard because these days people have access to so many different ways of learning how to be interviewed. I remember when I was going for job interviews I had no idea other than I knew that I had to wear a nice suit, be well groomed and polite and be thankful if I got the job. Now, when you interview people it's so much harder because they've been trained to tell you what you want to hear.

I've made mistakes. I've fallen for it. It is gut instincts. I've learned that you can generally work them out if you throw in a question not related to the role.

Something along the lines of, "If you were in a fire, what would be the first thing that you'd go and get in the house before you left it?" Psychologically, whatever their answer is, you can generally tell what sort of person they are and whether or not they have the same values of the company and are going to fit the culture.

It's a work in progress and I'm not perfect at it and neither are my managers. We still struggle with this and we still have days that we employ great people and they've been with us forever and we have other days where we employ great people and they don't last. In the last six or seven years, we haven't had a resignation and that is the key. If you retain you don't have to employ regularly.

When an Employee Doesn't Work Out

We have had employees who haven't worked out. A young woman came to me with very good qualifications. She said all the right things in the interview. After about three or four weeks into the job, she came to me and said, "I don't think I can cope with this job. I thought I had amazing experience. Now, being in your company, I realize that I just don't have what I thought I had."

We have such experienced staff that sometimes when people leave their comfort zone, if they've worked somewhere a long time and they're the top in their field in that organization, when they work somewhere else they want to go back to where they weren't being challenged.

I don't get caught up in salary competition. If someone comes to me and says, "I've been offered a job and they're giving me another $10,000," I say, "Great. Go and take it." I'm not going to get caught up in giving them more money to stay. That sends a bad message. If I felt they were worth 10 grand more why hadn't I paid them 10 grand more?

Best not to be manipulated into giving them a pay raise. Generally you find that if you do that, they leave anyway. They're not there for the true commitment. They're just there for the money. That doesn't work long term. It's okay to have people leave because you haven't matched their salary request.

Another management rule with staff is not to be too involved in their personal life. I've learned a lot of lessons around that. A staff member had terrible personal problems. Her child had an accident and she had no money to pay the hospital bills, so I gave her paid time off. I loaned her money and gave her a salary advance to pay the hospital bills and when she came back to work she thought she had the control.

She kept telling me all about the personal issues. There were always problems. She was making big mistakes, costing us huge amounts of money. I'd call her in and she would say, "I haven't slept because he's still sick." She knew because I had children I would be sensitive to her situation.

After six months I terminated her and I learnt a lesson of not becoming involved in staff's personal issues to the extent that you make poor decisions for your business.

Some Employee Success Surprises:

I had a staff member whom I met with weekly during the three-month probation period. This particular member of staff was not stepping up to her role. During those three months I told her what she needed to do, otherwise we'd have to part ways.

I've done that in the past and it hasn't worked, but this young woman said that she wanted to make it work and that she wanted the job. She completely turned around and was one of my best producers.

The advice here is you have to be honest with employees and be hard on them in the beginning. If they take it and they blossom even better. If they don't, they're not right for the company.

A Fish Rots from the Head

In any business, not just travel, the reality is that if the person at the top is not doing all they can to run a successful business, being a strong leader, walking the talk, being transparent, being honest, acting on their values, which are generally the values of the company, it filters down.

For example, if the owner of the business or the manager goes out for a long lunch every Friday, that's going to be okay for everyone else to do. When someone else does that and that manager or boss then says, "You're not entitled to go out on a Friday and not come back to the office," the other employees start to wonder why it's okay for the manager but not for them.

You are being watched all the time by your staff. When I walk into the office in the morning I tell myself that whatever's going on in my life does not matter when I walk through that door. I am happy. I say "Good morning, how are you?" to every individual staff member and take the time to go to each of their desks.

The fish rots from the head. If you're the head you have to take that responsibility and ensure you walk the talk if you want to have a successful company and have staff that respect you.

Employees Must Respect You and What You Are Doing

Having the respect from your staff is key to success. You have to look at yourself. If I have stages where we've lost a lot of staff in a short period of time, I ask myself, "What's happening here? What's going on that everyone's resigning? What are we doing that's losing people?" If things are not working in your business you have to look at yourself because you're the leader and you are leading the business. If you respect your staff and treat them as you want to be treated, that's the beginning of earning respect.

TIPS

---

1. Regular Meetings with Staff

We have a number of different meeting scenarios. We have a fortnightly staff meeting that is just a half an hour, 8:30 to 9:00 every second Wednesday. The agenda is sent out on Tuesday. It's to inform staff about whatever is going on. Then each department has a huddle, three minutes, where each team member shares their good news, what they are working on and what they are stuck on.

All of our main departments do these huddles and they work well. We also have annual evaluations with staff. We also ask questions—what do you think we should start doing, keep doing, and stop doing? Asking staff opinions helps with engagement to the business.

2. Reward Employees: A Happy Staff Equals Happy Clients (10-year diamond club)

We have a lot of long-term staff. Five years ago I wondered what we could do to reward them when they got to 10 years. The travel industry can be transient. I wanted to put something in place that after working with Spencer Travel for 10 years employees get a reward for their loyalty to the company. I love diamonds. The travel industry is predominantly female. I thought we could do a diamond club.

I worked out if a one-carat diamond costs $10,000, it's only a thousand dollars a year of investment in that staff member. If you put $1,000 aside for each staff member, it isn't a lot of money when you get to 10 years. It's not a huge investment if you break it down. We now have five members of staff with a one carat diamond.

If you have a plan for rewarding your staff when the staff member gets to 10 years, it gets picked up by the travel media. Everyone in the travel industry knows that we give a one carat diamond. People want to work for us. It promotes us. The staff feel truly rewarded and one to two years out they get excited about the prospect of getting a diamond. I start asking them a year before, "What do you want? Do you want a ring? Do you want earrings? Do you want a necklace? Start looking at jewelry shops." They get excited about that. It's a really positive way of saying thank you for your service.

I think 10 years is a huge commitment to a company and worthy of a diamond.

3. How to Keep the Passion Alive with Your Employees

We create a painted picture at the end of the year that we present to the staff in January. It's about the vision for next year, how we want to look in December of the upcoming year. We even put funny things on there like we'd love Hugh Jackman to be sitting at the desk booking an airline ticket with us.

It's putting a vision out there for the staff so that we're all on the same page about what we want out of the business.

Then in January and February we put together a business plan, which is very different from the painted picture because the business plan is the plan, not so much the vision. I present that to the staff in late February for the year ahead.

Because I meet with them twice a year, we incorporate that vision and that plan into our meetings. It's kept fresh throughout the whole year. We encourage everyone to constantly talk about the vision and the plan.

We have the painted picture on our communal kitchen pin board so they look at it while eating lunch. It's forefront in their mind and it keeps them motivated.

CHAPTER 9:

Clients: How to Find Them and Keep Them

The best way to find new clients is word of mouth. When people know you are doing a superb job, they want to use your services. It's the same in every business—referral and word of mouth. Having a business development manager works if you've got the right one. They have to understand your business and its culture to be able to sell the business to prospective clients.

As far as clients are concerned, it's about that relationship and being honest, having open communication, and acknowledging their needs. We go in not with a one-size-fits-all mindset. We're very open to adjusting our offer depending on what the client really needs. We try to understand their business as opposed to just saying, "This is what we do." We like to understand what they need and then tailor our services to them.

Advertising and Promotion

Advertising has not worked with corporate travel in the past. People don't look for a corporate travel management company in the Yellow Pages or in a magazine. We've tried it all. We do a lot of SEO, search engine optimization, on our website. That has worked with being on the first page of Google when people type in business travel or corporate travel.

We get a lot of inquiries through our website. Advertising online has not worked. Facebook has not worked. LinkedIn maybe a little but not hugely. The whole social media side I don't think wins you clients. It gives you brand awareness but doesn't necessarily win you new clients.

We have used Twitter for the space tickets, which might be more about people understanding that they can buy tickets to space as opposed to where to buy them. Retail travel is very different. Getting clients for retail travel, again, is very much word of mouth. Advertising does work for retail travel but not corporate.

What does work is if you put yourself out as an expert. I employed a PR agency a year ago and that resulted in having articles about me in *The Financial Review* and *The Australian* and different business magazines. I've won new business because people have read about me and my business.

Other business owners are reading them and other CEOs and owners or MDs are reading those magazines and they become inspired by my story or by something I said.

Finding and Pursuing New Clients

Persistence is key in gaining new business. Some time ago I'd been given a tip that a certain producer wasn't happy with his existing travel agency, so I called him. Every time I called, he wasn't available or couldn't take my call. That went on for some time. Then I was working late one night and decided to call him about 7:00 p.m. because I thought he would likely pick up the phone because everyone else would have left the office. I called and he picked up the phone. He said he'd seen all of my messages and he'd been meaning to call me back but he never got the chance. He said he would let me come in and meet with him purely because of my persistence.

That was the beginning of the entertainment area of travel for us. We did the Qantas commercial with his production company and then from there it was just word of mouth. Lots of other production companies started to use us.

That was about 20 years ago when I was trying to grow the business I was working for before I started my own in 1998. Part of my role was to manage and also grow that business and get new clients. This producer followed me when I started my own company.

The lesson here for other small businesses is to never give up. Keep persisting and don't get disillusioned by people not taking your calls. There's a fine line between stalking and being persistent. If you're ringing three times a day, that's stalking. If you're ringing once every couple of days, that's just being persistent.

Word of mouth is really significant. Initially, in the beginning of my business, word of mouth was how I built the business by doing a good job and staying connected with the clients. The lesson is if you do a good job in one industry, you can win more business by being an expert in that field.

Different Types of Clients Need to Be Treated Differently

We go above and beyond for our clients quite often. There was a very wealthy American woman who was so frightened after 9/11 that she didn't want to fly commercial, so we had to find a way to get her from one part of the world across to Asia. We had to take her via the military points because that was the only way we could get her from this particular point to another point in the world without going through commercial airports. That was a real challenge, but we pulled it off and it all worked, but we had to get quite a few different options and different quotes. In the end, we did offer her the whole cabin in first class, which would have been cheaper than the way that she actually chose. We definitely pull rabbits out of hats. That was one of the most expensive fares we have ever booked.

We had to fly her using private jets and military air bases. There is a lot of money involved in taking civilians through military air bases. It requires a lot of organization and is very expensive. We proved to the company and the client that we are prepared to do whatever it takes to go above and beyond. For clients like that we can make the impossible happen.

It comes back to relationships and the consultants. I have a consultant who is exceptionally good at high-end leisure travel. Anyone who comes in who wants a beautiful 30-day, high-end trip through Europe, she will look after them. We've got entertainment clients who do commercials and they deal with consultants who like to do large group travel with lots of changes. There are certain types of consultants who can handle the sort of business that changes constantly.

Then there are certain corporate clients who are high maintenance. In these cases, you need a relaxed consultant who can handle being yelled at if they can't get seat 1A. Then you've got the corporate client who just wants a Sydney-London-Sydney, and don't even talk to me and ask me how my day is. I just want you to make the booking and not interact with me.

Getting to know the client is key. We take time to understand what their needs and personalities are, and match them with the right consultant. I have had disasters where I've matched a certain type of client with a certain type of consultant and the consultant is permanently in tears.

I have had times that I've had to sack a client because they've been so rude to my staff, which I won't tolerate. If they're using bad language and screaming at them, saying, "You're absolutely useless," we don't need a client like that.

We had one very profitable corporate account but the Managing Director was a bully. Instead of letting his PA handle his travel, which would have been easier, he always got involved and was just plain rude to the consultant.

This particular consultant is in her 50s, very well-traveled, very good at what she does, and strong. But she was in tears. I rang him and said, "I'm sorry, but I think you need to find another travel agent." He was appalled and started yelling at me as well. I said, "I'm sorry. I just can't accept people yelling at my staff and swearing at them."

Even though that account was very profitable, I had to make that decision. Again, it comes back to our culture. That's not the way that I would expect my staff to be treated, and I earned respect from my staff for sacking the client over his behavior and not just looking at the bottom line. Ensure you live your values in business.

Going Above and Beyond

We had a client who got on a flight in New York, sitting on the tarmac, and the TV screen wasn't working. He phoned us and said, "My TV screen is not working. Can you sort it out?" We get a lot of clients that ring us from the hotel room and say, "I don't have any towels in my room. Can you sort it out?"

We had a celebrity client who was very unhappy because people were bothering him for autographs when he landed in Hong Kong. The PA called us and said, "We can't have this. This is appalling and you need to stop it." Then when he landed in Bangkok, we had one person to meet him and hardly ever looked at him. Then the PA called us and said, "He's upset because no one acknowledged him." Sometimes you can't win.

Some of the requests that we get are quite bizarre. You just have to go with it and offer the service. It's definitely about going above and beyond.

Helping clients out of difficult scenarios is also something that we're good at. We had a client who went to Greece and went on a quad bike with her boyfriend. They were in Santorini. It was a beautiful hot day. Of course they were wearing shorts, sandals as well as no helmet. The quad bike's brakes failed and it ran into a tree. The boyfriend was driving and his spleen and lungs were crushed. We had to organize to get him, first, from Santorini to Athens, and then in hospital for weeks and weeks in Athens, and then home from Athens.

We had another awful instance where one of our corporate clients was in New York and his son was killed. We had to get him back. People don't realize when you're in travel, you have to move mountains sometimes. And we do. That's why we have long-term satisfied clients. In any business you need to make a difference to your clients and build your services to the point that they can't do without you.

Competition is Fierce

In the marketplace, the competition is strong. We sell ourselves as being the best. We can save client's money on airfares rather than with the service fees. That's the misconception in the marketplace. A lot of our competitors go out and discount service fees as opposed to showing the true savings that they can save them in travel costs, not diluting your own income.

The internet competition was huge five years ago but clients are coming back now because people are time poor. They realize that they're not the expert and that having their PAs make their bookings doesn't work. The domestic market has turned around to using travel agents rather than the internet. In any business it is vital to remember not to give up on what worked previously.

We find now that a lot of clients will research online, but bring in the research to the office and say, "This is what I'd like to do. What do you think? Can you book it?" They're not feeling as confident about booking it online. They feel more confident coming to an actual person rather than using an unknown website.

In five years' time people are going to be even more time poor. It comes back to choice. When you think about how much information is on the Internet if you typed in "Hotel in Athens," there are too many search results. People are going to just get bewildered by the choices and options that come up.

They say, "I'll check TripAdvisor," which is where people will go to if there's too much choice and they're not sure. They'll be guided by TripAdvisor. There are always going to be things online that people will try. Long term, it will be a research tool rather than a booking tool. People, at the end of the day, like human interaction and knowing that they can call if something goes wrong.

You must recognize and reward your clients, just as you do with your staff. We have a client retention scheme that we put in place that works very well for us. When PAs leave a particular corporation and they show up somewhere else, they'll remember that

Spencer Travel really looked after them personally and sent them a birthday present and took them to a movie.

You must be forefront in their minds.

Clients Who Have Special Needs and Disability Holidays

In addition to the employees who work for me, I also have contractors who come to me with their book of business. One of the independent contractors, Simon, specializes in tours for disabled people.

Simon came up with the concept of disability holidays. I've supported him through that and helped him with the ways to make it work.

Through Simon we offer fully supported and escorted holidays for people with an intellectual disability, mobility challenges, and mental health issues or acquired brain injuries. Simon has been employed in hospitality, airline, car hire and travel industries for over 20 years, and meeting with disability support workers who showed a keen interest in taking clients on a experiential holiday was the start of our Supported Holidays.

We wanted to offer memorable, fun holidays while at the same time keeping them affordable. We have spent many years traveling to Bali, and came up with an itinerary for clients who have disabilities or clients who require assistance. We have been able to successfully take three separate groups to experience what Bali has to offer—culture, fun parks, Animal Safari Zoo, and much more. We have support personnel who are all highly experienced and trained disability support staff, including a registered nurse. This expertise, coupled with fun-loving people, is the perfect recipe for a great holiday and I am very pleased to have someone like Simon manage these. It gives us a way to make a difference in an unexpected but very meaningful way.

Recently, he read an article in the local paper about a woman who has a disability. She had always wanted to go to Hamilton Island. It was one of her life dreams.

So between the both of us, we managed to get her a couple of tickets, accommodation, and some spending money. When she found out, she was crying on the phone. She couldn't believe that anyone would do something like that for her.

We really try to do things that are going the extra mile for people. We don't just read an article and say, "Oh, how sad." It is part of our culture as a company to care about others and to do what we can to help.

It is important in business to support new markets but also to not always be thinking commercially; give back where you can.

CHAPTER 10:

Managing Business and Personal Life

"Having it all is definitely doable, but it has to be managed."

When you have a business it can totally consume your life, but you have to be very vigilant in making sure that you leave time for yourself, your family, and your friends. Having it all is definitely doable, but it has to be managed.

People think, "I'll just work 24 hours a day and I'll be successful," but that's not just what makes you successful. What makes you successful is balance in life, happiness, and being healthy.

To find that balance, you have to consciously make time. I'm an extreme planner, which my husband actually hates at times, but I think he appreciates it secretly, because we do have balance in our lives. My weeks are very busy, but it's all completely to plan. If I have to do exercise, it's in my calendar, and anything in my calendar, I do. I don't cancel things unless it's life or death.

It is all about time management and planning. And being very strong about saying "No." For example, my calendar will have at 5:30 "Exercise" and if that's in there, that's what I do, and so on, throughout the day. If it's one of my child's concert at school that I have to go to, that'll go into my work calendar. I have the one calendar.

It's being really strict on yourself and working off your calendar. What's in your calendar is what you do. And then, the other side of it is allotting the time for family as opposed to the business. I have Mondays off from the office. I'll do e-mails at home. But mostly, it's Monday for the family, doing what I have to do with the kids and being involved in the school as well as anything domestic.

And then Saturday, Sunday, I don't work. I might look at my phone and look at the odd e-mail, but I definitely never sit down at a desk or go into the office. Friday night is shut down from the office until I go back in there on Tuesday. I get to have three days solidly with the family. Being present is enormously important.

When I'm at home with them, I'm at home with them. I'm not trying to do 50,000 other things. There are times when there are problems at the office or with a client and I will have to be on the phone. But, generally, I've set the business up now so that it is handled by other people.

Ensuring balance gives you the best of both worlds.

How Managing Both Evolved with Changing Circumstances

Pre-children, I lived and breathed the business because it was my child. My husband came into the business three years into it. We both lived and breathed the business. We were quite strict about having time out for holidays. We would do two or three breaks from the business a year, which I think is really important as a married couple in a business.

I remember being there till all hours of the night and not really having much of a life. But it was also in the stage of building the business. I was the one doing everything from issuing a ticket to hiring staff and cleaning the toilets.

In the beginning, if you're starting a business as a mother already, it would be difficult. You'd really have to have great support and have people you could delegate to. Looking back to the first four years of starting, running and growing the business without children, I was able to do that because I only had the business to concentrate on.

Building a new business is all consuming, so ensure you have a very strong network and support team.

Keeping Up with Changes at Home and in the Office

I don't mind change, but I hate my schedule being mucked up. On a day to day basis, if something happens that's not locked into my calendar, I get quite anxious about it. But then I get to work rearranging what needs to be changed. I can do it within five minutes. But, initially, I do get upset.

For instance, if one of my children is sick and I have a meeting at 8:00 a.m. and the nanny doesn't come until 1:00 p.m. because my kids are school-age, I find that very stressful but I just have to manage it. I have a very supportive husband who understands that I'm the key person in the business. As much as I'm the mother, he can step in when he needs to.

My husband Edwin will say, "Don't worry, I'll just sort it out. You go." It's about having that support. As Edwin puts it, "We can't both work at full power. It doesn't work for our family."

Ensure you have a fallback person both at home and in the business.

Winding Down and Gearing up: Going from Home to the Office and Back

To give me the energy to get through the workday, I exercise five mornings a week, with Saturday and Sunday off. If I don't exercise at that usual time, I start to feel tired around 3:00 p.m. When I've exercised in the morning, for an hour or 45 minutes, I don't get that lag of energy at all.

I love doing outside exercises as opposed to inside a gym. Walking by the ocean and looking out is a great way to start your day and have time away from everyone. A lot of my best ideas come to me at that time. If I'm scheduled to make a speech for some event, that's when I create it in my head. That's the time that I really have nothing around me other than nature.

I don't watch TV. When all the jobs are finished, I go to bed and read. I would love to read a trashy novel, but most of the time it is based around business or travel. I read a lot of travel magazines at night to see what's going on in the industry and about new destinations and products. That's how I wind down at night.

Everyone has to have a way to wind down; exercise, sports, hobbies or reading. You can't be on high energy all the time. It is not sustainable.

Pay Yourself a Salary so You Don't Start Begrudging the Business

In the beginning, when you start a business, you should pay yourself a salary. When a lot of entrepreneurs first start a business, they think they can't pay themselves a salary until they make some money.

But the reality is, you're the most important person in that business. And you need to have the energy to grow that business and make it work. If you're not paying yourself a salary, you might start begrudging the business because you are going to feel you are doing all the work for nothing.

It's very much a psychological scenario in your head that you think you're working so hard, but you're getting nothing back, even though it is your own business. So, even if you get a loan from the bank or you sell shares to start the business, from day one, you should pay yourself. Even if it's $100 or $200, it's saying that A) You're doing this hard work, but you are getting some sort of a return; and B) The business is paying you back for what you're doing.

If you're not paying yourself, why are you in business? You have bought yourself a job. And a job that you're not getting paid for. The most satisfying part of that is as the business grows, you start paying yourself more.

I remember when I started the business, I was paying myself maybe $200 a week, a really minimal amount. And then as the business started to grow, the accountant would say "Okay, I think we can increase your pay." Or, "As it is even bigger now, we can take dividends." You feel a sense of achievement.

CHAPTER 11:

Working with a Spouse

Your spouse can be your teammate, but you have to decide right away who is going to be the boss. I started the business myself. Edwin was in quite a stressful role of project manager for constructing large houses. He was working very long hours and I was working very long hours. As my business grew, three years into it, I realized that I needed somebody who could handle the infrastructure—IT, phones, where to put another desk, how does it get all wired up? That is not my area.

I said to my husband "We never ever see each other. We're newlyweds." (We got married the same year that I started the business.) "Maybe you should come into this business and help with the infrastructure and the IT." And he agreed.

Be Clear-Cut with the Employees, too, about Who Is Boss and Who Does What

We then sat down and had a business discussion about "How

would this work?" "What are the guidelines for working together?" We put together strict guidelines. Number one was that I was boss and he would have nothing to do with running the staff, but we would make the big decisions together.

The staff would also know that he was a director of the business, but they weren't to go to him for any decisions. That's another area that can be difficult for employees when they're working for a husband and wife team. It's almost like children, you get a "no" from mum, so you'll go to dad to get a "yes."

The other guideline is we never bring our personal life into the office. If we have an argument in the morning, we need to sort that out before we walk into the office.

That takes a lot of discipline. In 16 years, there probably was only one time when we have had to close the door in my office and sort out an issue that we had personally. But no one knew as we did it privately.

Dealing with How Outsiders See You and Your Spouse as a Team

About six or seven years ago, Edwin and I went to a meeting at the bank. The bankers focused completely on Edwin. They completely ignored me and talked to him about him about the money, what we were trying to do, how we were going to do it and the interest rates. They never even looked at me until Edwin got a moment where he could interrupt them and said, "Just so you know, Penny's actually the boss. Not me."

The banker looked at Edwin and said, "Oh. I assumed you were the managing director of the business."

He immediately assumed that the husband was the key person in the business.

The message here is to always ensure that you talk to people about your position as opposed to letting people just assume that you're not the key decision maker in the business.

We are always asked, "Who's the boss at home?" And I always turn around and say, "Well, of course Edwin's boss at home."

Always be transparent and clear in your roles.

Upsides to Having a Spouse as Your Partner

I will ask Edwin's advice and opinion. His opinions are valid and he sees things differently. He's very logical, where I might be more emotional about something. I'm a bit more flamboyant with money, whereas he's a lot more sensible.

I'm a great believer that if you put it out there, the money will come. I've been like that all my life and it is true because I've worked hard. Whereas Edwin's a lot more cautious and would rather wait and see. He reins me in quite a bit, but it works. I respect what he says and he respects my decisions.

It's worked over time and we have grown into our roles. Respecting each other and your differences is the key to working together.

How to Keep the Office in the Office and Not Bring Work Issues Home

Keeping home and office separate is not easy, but important. I have a 35-minute drive to the office. That 35-minute drive winds me down and allows me to think about what's happened during the day. By the time I get home, I'm a lot more relaxed and able to switch into family mode.

Ensuring you talk about the business at set times and allowing for other conversation at home helps with keeping the two separate.

Pluses of Working with a Spouse

1. You are in it together.

2. You're a maker of your own destiny together.

3. You share the same vision and goals.

4. You have different talents in different areas of the business.

5. You have flexibility with your lifestyle.

Downsides to Having a Spouse as a Partner

1. Keeping your business and personal life separate.

2. Seeing each other all the time (this can be a positive as well).

3. Business relying on you both.

4. The business being your only source of income.

5. Familiarity of knowing each other's weaknesses.

Handling Logistics if Your Partner is Your Spouse

We don't drive into the office together or drive home together. One will drop off the kids, one will go to the office, depending on the day. I'll arrive at a certain time, Edwin will arrive at a different time, and we leave at different times. We work at separate ends of the office.

Unless we have a meeting, we don't see each other. He's involved in infrastructure, which is not my area. So, whereas I am in my office or in meetings all day, he is running around.

I've only ever known the travel industry. Edwin has been in the building industry all his life and only been in the travel industry now for ten years. As an outsider looking in, he comes up with lots of different ideas that I probably wouldn't think of. He brings in fresh ideas about different ways to do things.

He came up with the idea of each employee having two screens. We were the leaders in the industry in that. We gained publicity about that and people would come to our office to have a look. So, he's very good at looking outside the square and bringing new ideas to me.

You must have equality with the perks of the business. For example, when educationals or conferences are offered, Edwin is not included in those as they are for selling staff only. If I was to send him on an educational over a staff member, this would be very bad business practice and result in a lot of unhappy and resentful staff. Edwin only goes on trips that we are invited to as Directors of the business and we tell the staff this is a personal invitation. Transparency is the key.

Wise and Unwise Partner Choices

My advice is never employ family or friends in business. They can be hard to manage. They can take advantage. Just because you like them as a person and you know them socially doesn't necessarily mean their work ethic is the same as yours.

The same with family—bringing family into your business brings a lot of other scenarios as well. Family can feel they have more of a right to the business and to the way you run it and that they have more of a say because they're family.

I employed a family member in my business for a short period of time in the early days, maybe for a couple of weeks to help out, in situations like data entry or when the receptionist was away. I'd call family or a friend in for a couple of weeks. But I wouldn't employ a family or friend long term.

It's very hard when you have to reprimand family or friends and it's very hard to get rid of them.

Your existing staff can find it difficult to have your family and friends working in the business. They feel that they're favored or got the job because of who they are rather than their skills and capabilities.

Be cautious employing family or friends.

CHAPTER 12:

How to Win Awards to Put the Spotlight on Your Business

Winning awards doesn't just happen. You need to plan for it.

Six years ago, I started putting a plan together to enter certain travel agency awards to win best travel agency, best consultant, or best manager. Then, as we won those types of awards, I felt it was important to go into awards around my profile—businesswomen awards, for example. I also went for other entrepreneurial awards. You need to be strategic about what awards will suit you at what time in your business.

It's being aware of where you are in your business and what you feel you need to grow and to what audience. In the beginning of my business it was about getting our profile out into the travel industry. We then started going broader and submitting to bigger business awards. We won the city of Sydney business award for travel and tourism. We went out into broader markets and profiling myself, that's when you start looking at businesswomen awards.

It is a lot of work doing award submissions and also presenting to the judges if you get to the finalist stage.

When you prepare a submission and look back over the year, you realize how much you've accomplished. It's a rewarding process to do the submission even though it can take time, and again, that's where you come back to a point in your business where you're working on it, not in it, allowing you to have the time to look at what your business needs.

The incredible thing about winning awards is that the staff get energized by it. If we win an award, the next day when you come into the office everyone is so excited and so proud and that builds your culture.

Three years ago, the day came that I was meant to present to the judges for the best corporate agency award at 1:00 p.m. I had spent months working on the submission. Around 10:00 a.m. on the day of the presentation, I was reading through everything to prepare myself. Our nanny called to say my three-year-old son had had an accident. I rushed to the hospital and after many tests he showed signs of coherence. I had to leave to present to the judges.

I took a taxi to the presentation. I took a huge amount of breaths and walked in and gave the presentation. I didn't say anything about what I'd just been dealing with because I didn't want the sympathy vote.

I went into that zone and then went back to the hospital. It was all a complete blur. I said to all my staff, "We are not going to win, there's no way." About six weeks later we found out we won. You have to be committed to the cause and do your best no matter what.

Another instance where we submitted an award under very trying circumstances happened that same year. My husband Edwin always helps a lot with the submissions. He's very logical. When I type away, it's as though I'm talking, which is not ideal. I do all of that preliminary work and then he comes in and tidies it up and makes it presentable.

He had open-heart surgery in May and we did the submission in June. He came out of the hospital, sat at the desk and went through what I had written and did what he had to do on his end for me. Both of us are very committed and focused, and what needs to be done, gets done. If you want to be involved in award submissions you have to be committed.

The Australian Federation of Travel Agents award has always been one that I've liked to be a part of because it's very well recognized within the travel industry. To be the winner four times in a row, and entered into the Hall Of Fame, is huge within the travel industry. It also means a lot to clients. When you can say we won the national travel industry award for best corporate agency four times in a row, people are impressed. Any award you win is good for business.

When my Business Development Manager visits prospective clients and there's another agency that's trying to undercut, she will sell our awards. When you're winning awards consecutively every year, you can't undersell your own product, because you are seen as the best so it's important to be award winning; it means that customers will pay more for you because you are the best.

If you promote your awards, it has to be relevant and current. I looked at a proposal of a company recently. Their awards were for 2003, 2004, 2007. I asked about their current awards. There's no point in telling me about an award you got six years ago. What's happened in the last six years? It's crucial to market that the awards are current.

It comes back to strategy and planning. Every year when we do our business planning, we sit down and work out what awards we will submit; it's very strategic and for lots of reasons. It's not just about the clients seeing you as the best and therefore paying more for your services. It's about having good staff wanting to work for you and stay with you. This can save on recruitment fees, which is an added benefit of winning prestigious awards.

The staff also like to apply for awards. One of my staff just entered an award for a scholarship. She had to put together a submission and then present it to judges. While she didn't win the scholarship, she said that she got so much out of the process and has grown from it. It's addictive. Once you start, you see the results and you get quite excited about the prospect of what award is next.

I did a submission for Telstra business women of the year and was a finalist, but it took three or four months to put together. The process can be daunting.

My advice is to start small. If you do want to win awards, start with a small award, whether it be a local community award or an industry award. Take baby steps and also start preparing yourself by being confident with presenting.

Once you start the process, think of going to ToastMasters or get some sort of training in public speaking; you need to have the confidence to be able to stand up and present. Confidence comes with experience, but if you go to courses that focus on public speaking, you can learn different ways and processes to help with nerves.

Using a PR agency can help with the award submission process. When engaging the PR agency, you need to know your objective, what you want to achieve. A year ago I felt like we needed to get our brand out in the broader market. We are very well known within the travel industry but as far as the market, which translates into possible new clients and consumers, we aren't well known. That was my key objective to have brand awareness in the broader market. You need to ensure you know your key objectives before hiring a PR Agency.

CHAPTER 13:

Giving Back

While you want to help everyone, and you get asked three or four times a day, you need to have a plan about who you support when it comes to charity. First of all, what we do every year is donate 50 cents per invoice to a charity that's chosen by staff.

We choose the charity through a voting system. At the staff meetings everyone will propose a charity that they'd like to support. Sometimes a lot of them will choose the same charity, other times there will be six different charities to choose from. I research those charities, because a lot of the time we've got to make sure that, A) it's a viable charity, and B) our money is not going to be used mainly in administration fees. We research the charities and then come back to the next staff meeting to explain each charity that everyone has chosen and then we have a vote. The charity that gets the most votes is the charity for the year that we support.

You will find everyone has in their own mind what they want

to support, whether it be animals, children, elderly people. It is what's affected everybody in their life. We recently supported a charity called Bear Cottage, where terminally ill children go for respite so their parents can have a break from caring for them. The parents live in the house as well, they bring in people to do massages for the mother or give back to the parents who have been caring for their terminally ill child.

Volunteering Is Another Form of Charity Support.

This year we cooked for a whole day in an industrial kitchen for the charity OZ Harvest and made huge amounts of meals for the homeless. Everyone felt they were giving back and they enjoyed the day. We love to give back and we'll continue to do that. This year we are looking at helping children by going to paint a school or build a playground.

We have worked with Kayak for Kids, where we kayaked Sydney Harbor. We raised money for handicapped children and the staff loved doing that.

TIME, the Travel Agency Mentor Experience that I founded, is definitely giving back to the industry. I helped to start a charity with my nephew called Spencer Swim Safe, which is sending swimming instructors to underprivileged areas of the world where children can't swim. We have done a program in the Philippines and one up in far north Queensland, teaching aboriginal children how to swim.

Give and you will receive. Being involved in charities and giving back should be part of your strategic plan.

Sustaining a Giving Plan

To keep up the charitable giving, you must remain profitable. We put a portion of our profits into the community in some form or another whether it be the 50 cents or in other ways. Sometimes we can do more, like charity balls that I can take the staff to.

The staff definitely like the fact that it's not all about just bringing money into the bank. It's about giving back. They feel that they're working for a company that has a commitment to helping others. What the staff like is they see that it's in the budget. We talk about it regularly and discuss it in staff meetings. Also, we always do some sort of charity-type event at our staff conferences.

It comes back to our culture, which is about giving back. That's actually in our culture statement and staff do respond well to that. They feel like they're working for a company that has values and morals and does what they say.

CHAPTER 14:

Have an Exit Strategy Right from the Start

I became aware of the importance of having an exit plan in place sooner rather than later around the same time I was being mentored. Both the mentor and the coach taught me about looking ahead and looking at where I want to go and planning for that. Specifically, the coach talked a lot about succession planning. It's great to plan for 10 years within your business and say, "This is where I want to be in 10 years," but the idea of actually exiting your business, which you have no idea about when you're starting a business, needs to be addressed.

I've learned from having done mergers and acquisitions with business owners who are tired of the business that it's better to plan your succession 10 or even 15 years before you actually want to do it. This way you've got the energy to make it happen as opposed to doing it when you're sick of everything and can't be bothered. If your exit strategy is to sell the business to achieve the most amount of money for your business, you have to plan for it and implement the necessary changes to make the business viable for sale.

I started to put together an exit plan after being in business for a couple of years. The third year, I had a succession plan workshop with my coach and we planned the next 10 years of how I was going to make my business viable. Not that I wanted to necessarily sell; it was around making the business viable for sale. If a buyer came along and offered you $6 million for your business," would you be ready for that?

It's hard to think about that when you're two years into the business. You have no idea how much you're going to grow your business and at what point you are going to be happy with where you are. Even now, it's hard to even think about what figure I would want for my business if I decided to sell. Two years in, we started to discuss it. Five years in, I started making a plan for it and I've stuck mostly to that plan.

First, you need to look at why someone would buy a business. There's no point in having a database of 1,000 people if half of them are dead or no longer using your services. The database is key to the sale of your business. Having the right people in the right place. I have spent the last 10 years doing this.

A lot of my staff have been with me for 10-plus years and that was my plan, to have people long term in my business. I could groom them to become a part of the management team that would eventually take over if I wanted to sell to them or spend less time in the business or sell to an outsider.

When people look for a business to buy, they look at these areas. In addition to the database, the financials must show that you've been profitable for the last three years.

Another piece of advice about succession planning is not to have your name on the door. I thought long and hard about that for a few years because obviously my name is Penny Spencer and my business is called Spencer Travel and now Spencer Group of Companies, but I built the brand Spencer as opposed to the brand Penny Spencer. We have a profile now. I know people book with Spencer Travel because of our reputation and brand, not because of me. This makes the brand sellable.

You must take yourself out of the business, not being the key person the clients deal with. That was what I set out to do 11 years ago.

You will find it hard when you start a business because it's your baby. I always equate it to a child. You start it off as a baby, you nurture it, look after it, and you don't want to hand it over to anyone. As it gets a bit older, like your child, you send them off to school. It's sort of the same with business. After about five years, you think, "Now I can hand over a little bit." Then as time goes by 10, 11, 12, 13 years, the business becomes not as reliant on you.

It takes time. You definitely have to be strong and not fall back into the easy "What you know best." I was good at being a travel consultant, but I had to learn to be better at being a businessperson if I wanted the business to succeed.

Planning for the Right Buyer

I love what I do. Every day I get up and I can't imagine ever not having my business.

I have just turned 50 and I've still got all the energy in the world, but in 10 years' time maybe I won't have that same energy for the business.

Finding the right buyer personality-wise is also hard. I know the sort of person or company I would like to buy my business. You want to sell it to good operators and you want your staff to be well looked after.

I have been on the other side and bought a few businesses, so I can see how easy it is to get carried away in changing the business to the way that you want it to be and that's difficult for the person who created the business.

When I sell and if I sell, and if it's to an outside buyer as opposed to my staff buying it, I wouldn't want to stay there and see the changes. Many businesses when they sell, the new owners want the existing owner to stay in the business for at least a year and contract them into being in the business for a period of time. This can be very difficult for all involved.

If it is a family business you are preparing to sell, you must take the emotion out of it. You have to look at the business purely as an object to sell. If the whole family is involved in the business, generally you find it is generational and it's handed down. But if it is sold, again, it's the emotion that gets people into trouble.

Everyone thinks that their business is worth more than it actually is. I come across this all the time because I'm always looking at businesses to buy. It's hard to agree on the price because of the emotions involved.

There are formulas with selling a business depending on the industry. You need to be aware of the formula for your own industry before you put the business on the market.

It's hard to know when you have little children what they'll grow up to be. Are they going to be entrepreneurial? They always say the first generation builds a business, the second generation grows it, and the third generation spends the money.

It is important to keep in mind a key employee who might be interested in having a share in the business or eventually buying it. That key employee might be your manager, general manager, or another employee. If you can see their potential, you should be talking to them about the future.

For instance, my General Manager came to me two years into her career with us at Spencer Travel. I was doing personal goals and professional goals with her and I asked, "What's your long-term goal?" She replied "I want to be sitting in your seat." She was still working in domestic travel at the time and I replied, "Great. If that's what you want, that's where I'll take you." And that's where she is today.

I already had a succession plan, but I didn't have the person in mind because my business was so new, but once I realized that there was an employee within my business who wanted to go to that level, I groomed her for that. You need to identify the stars within your business and ensure you keep them interested.

One of the reasons I keep growing is I want my staff to continue to have new challenges so that they don't get bored and sick of the company and want to go somewhere else for challenges. Remain innovative if you want to retain a growing, innovative business by challenging and opening up opportunities for your staff.

When you have put a lot of hard work, blood, sweat, and tears into your business you want to ensure you get a certain amount of money. It's about how much money you want to live on. If it is a retirement scenario, you are selling your business because you are retiring, you need X amount of money to retire and to live for the next 20 years.

I've looked at businesses where it's not retirement. The owners want to get out of the business and do something else and they still have a different idea of the money that they should be getting. That's when you do your due diligence. I've done due diligence on businesses sometimes for six to eight months before I've given an offer or not given an offer.

It all goes back to if the business is sellable—if their clients aren't relying on that key person who is selling, if they have the right financials in place, have the right staff in place, if the staff will stay. The database, their IT equipment, what the technology is like, their productivity—there's so much that goes into that due diligence.

Sometimes I've looked at businesses that on the outside seem very successful and then you do your due diligence and find it's not worth buying.

I had a scenario where there was a company that was taken over by a large global company. They had an amazing staff with incredible knowledge. They had been in the industry 30-plus years. They serviced their clients above and beyond.

When the owner sold the business to a global company he obviously would have wanted his staff looked after. The big company didn't realize that those staff were key to keeping a lot of the clients. Those 12 staff ended up coming to me, and that global company lost a lot of business because of it. What they didn't look at was the individual staff's needs and wants.

The owner of the business, before he sold it, had one of the best travel companies in Australia. Everyone looked up to his company and he had a great reputation.

There are lots of lessons to learn. Being involved in mergers and acquisitions is another key to understanding succession planning. You can explore mergers and acquisitions or at least learn about them. Not necessarily to buy and sell, but at least to learn about the process so you understand all of the implications from the other side.

As for how much to tell employees when you are looking to sell your business, that can be difficult. Do you let your staff know that your business is on the market? Will they leave because they are nervous or do you keep it confidential and then let them know when it's sold? That is not an easy call to make.

My values are all around honesty and transparency. Not knowing but suspecting can lead to gossip and can create a worse picture for the staff if they hear it via another source. It's an individual case whether you tell your staff that you're selling. Most of the businesses that I have bought have not told their staff until the purchase has been finalized.

We all would like someone to walk in the door and offer us money, but the reality is that two, three years into your business, when you're busy growing the business, you need to take the time out to plan for the exit strategy.

Think about if someone gets sick or a family member dies, or the owner of the business sadly dies? Whatever the scenario, if there is a plan already in place, you can easily sell your business at any point in time.

An example is a business owner who lost a child and he lost all passion for his business. He was completely distraught and the business was just surviving but the staff were getting frustrated because they felt they had no leader and no guidance. They assumed the worst and everyone lost focus.

You can never plan for everything, but if you start early and have a strategy, you are always ready. I look at my plans every couple of years. When I do business planning annually, I always have the next stages for the succession plan in mind. I might plan to sell more shares, or promote the assistant manager so if I had to sell, I would have two very key managers in the business.

You have to plan for the unexpected. Things can change quickly in life and the business can be affected so never assume that it will always be business as usual.

CHAPTER 15:

Branching Out

Expanding comes back to understanding your market, what you're good at, and also the infrastructure within your business. If you're opening branches, everything should be managed at the head office. If you're opening multiple locations and they are not utilizing the infrastructure, you're duplicating everything per location.

If you branch out, think about the strategy. If you have separate offices running solely on their own and not utilizing your existing infrastructure, you have to be sure that each of those individual business are going to be profitable and able to run themselves.

I know with small travel agencies, generally they run themselves completely. That's why I have my locations utilizing the head office's infrastructure. We have an accounts team, an IT team, administration, and sales and marketing.

We love the entertainment travel side of our business and we would love to work in Los Angeles, but the reality is it's a whole different legislation in L.A. We'd have to get a different travel agent's license, different insurances. We don't know the market. If I had someone on the ground in L.A. who knows the market and has contacts, that might be different. But I wouldn't just go over to L.A., look for an office, and start a business. It's about having the right people in the right places.

Where to Seek out Advice

This kind of wisdom comes with experience. The longer you're in business, the more you realize a lot of people will give you advice, but it's not necessarily the right advice for your business. You need to be careful with the advisors that surround you and make sure you can trust them. I now have my key advisors being my accountant, my solicitor, and HR. It can take a while to get the right people.

You can be given the wrong advice that can cause failure in certain areas, and then you have to get up, brush yourself off, and go find another advisor.

We listened to all of the advice that our early accountant gave us. I was very busy building my business at the time and had my head down, not really thinking I needed to keep a handle on the financials. That's what the accountant was for. He would pass me the profit and loss and I'd look at the bottom line and say, "Oh there's profit there, good."

He made a very poor investment on our behalf, although we

agreed to it because he sold it to us so well, and we lost $100,000. This was year three in the business. That was a big learning curve for me. I had handed everything over to him from a financial point of view.

I realized, A) I hadn't kept a handle on what he was actually doing, and B) He was learning from us because he had never dealt with our industry before. We were guinea pigs. He was learning how our industry works. We were paying him a lot of money to learn about our industry.

Two lessons there. One is to still have a handle on what's happening with your advisors. You don't have to know everything about everything, but you need to know a little about a lot.

It is about education. After that happened I took a course on financials—learning how to read the P&L, a balance sheet, how to put a cash flow summary together—all of those basics that I hadn't understood.

Now I can question and ask, "Why is that there? Why did you put that in that area? Shouldn't it be in this area?"

It's also important to have advisors who understand your industry. Every industry is different.

Part of owning and running your own business is making mistakes and learning from them. Being an entrepreneur means learning from and building on experience. For the entrepreneur, problems are unrecognized opportunities.

MY THOUGHTS ON
STARTING A BUSINESS

- Don't be afraid. Step off the cliff.
- It will fluctuate and go up and down. Enjoy what you're doing and enjoy the roller coaster ride.
- It's not always going to be smooth; it's not always going to be bad. You will live and breathe it. You will love it and hate it. For me it has fulfilled my life and it's always with me. I love what I do, so I never work a day in my life.

Ten Tips for Running a Successful Business

1. Communicate with your staff on a daily basis.
2. Treat people as you would like to be treated.
3. Know a little about a lot.
4. Ensure you seek advice.
5. Look after yourself or else you cannot look after anyone else.
6. Learn from your mistakes.
7. Do as you say.
8. Say "Thank you." Reward and recognize. Not just your staff, also clients, suppliers. Anyone that helps you along the way.
9. Know your financials. Always know your cash position because cash is king.
10. Celebrate everything. Always make sure you take the time to celebrate what you've achieved.

Final Tip: Always dress for the job you want, not the job you have. *And* always wear lipstick, especially red; it exudes power and confidence.

ABOUT THE AUTHOR

I took my first plane trip when I was eight and I remember that feeling of excitement and wonderment. "What's going to happen when we land?" and, "What's the city going to be like?" I still have that when I travel. I think most people do. If you're going somewhere new, it's so exciting. I knew then that I wanted to work in the travel industry. At first I was thinking about being an air hostess, but as I got older, I realized that I wanted to be a travel agent, selling the dream to people.

The important thing is to love what you do. The passion for whatever business you are in has to be there. *If you want to be successful, you have to love what you do every day.* If you love what you do, you never work a day in your life. Even after thirty years, I still wake up excited about going to work.

Being in business can be like a roller coaster ride, and if you love what you do, you keep striving to get through the dizzying ups and downs. You might feel sick along the way wondering how you are going to get through. Loving what you do ensures you keep striving. I have learnt being successful comes in many forms and I hope you enjoy my journey.